SORRY

I HUMPED YOUR LEG

SORRY
I HUMPED Y♥UR LEG

(and Other Letters from Dogs Who Love Too Much)

Jeremy Greenberg

Andrews McMeel Publishing®

a division of Andrews McMeel Universal

Andrews McMeel Publishing
a division of Andrews McMeel Universal
1130 Walnut Street, Kansas City, Missouri 64106

www.andrewsmcmeel.com

www.jeremygreenberg.com

17 18 19 20 21 TEN 10 9 8 7 6 5 4 3 2 1

ISBN: 978-1-4494-8050-9

Library of Congress Control Number: 2016956803

Editor: Allison Adler
Art Director: Holly Swayne
Production Editor: Erika Kuster
Production Manager: Tamara Haus

ATTENTION: SCHOOLS AND BUSINESSES

Andrews McMeel books are available at quantity discounts with bulk purchase
for educational, business, or sales promotional use. For information,
please e-mail the Andrews McMeel Publishing Special Sales Department:
specialsales@amuniversal.com.

For Pursey, Estee, Seymour, Sophie,
Ms. Cate, Lewis, Dagny, Dobie,
and warmest of all, Uno.

Dear Pack Leader in a Paw Print–Covered Parka,

To answer your question, "No, Ladybug is not locked up." Ladybug's love for Pack Leader is no match for any backyard fence. Your love must be just as strong or you wouldn't have stacked the firewood next to the fence at the perfect basset hound–escape angle. Are we going skiing? Put me in your backpack so I can guard the beef jerky. Are you trying to photograph wildlife? I promise to bark at even the slightest noise so the animals know where to come get their pictures taken. Don't let the other human pack members put me back in the house. I'll easily bust out of any bathroom that doesn't have rounded knobs. And every dog's seen the YouTube video of the retired bomb sniffer demonstrating how to pop a kennel latch with a claw. Ladybug's love knows no constraint! I'm pretty sure if trapped on a balcony I could shimmy down the water drain. Nothing will stop me from making your day memorable.

There's a skunk in that bush who'd like to meet you,
Ladybug

There isn't a backyard fence in all the world
that could keep us apart
Doggie: Ladybug

Will you be my Pack Leader?
All the other humans are zombies
Puppy: Oreo

Dear Apocalypse-Surviving Pack Leader,

Seeing as you're the only human I've encountered who hasn't tried to eat my brains, I'm wondering if you'll be my forever human. I asked the first human I saw, but he was waking up from a long nap and just growled and hissed. However his friends were very eager to play chase. They surrounded me, and I was about to let them all pet me in hopes that it would improve the group's mood. But zombies must be oxytocin deficient, and I was nearly brain food. Fortunately one of their carnivorous colleagues accidentally bit into what was actually a haunted Halloween electronic jack-o'-lantern. It cackled and shot sparks but the distraction saved Oreo's stuff. Now you can be my forever human! If you're worried about vet bills, you can take comfort that forever isn't nearly as long as it used to be. Based on how the wall behind me is leaning under the pressure of 30,000 technically expired Pack Leaders, I'd estimate forever to be about thirteen minutes. Plenty of time to play fetch!

Please don't trade me for fuel,
Oreo

Dear Very Important Pack Leader,

I'm excited to have been chosen as your new personal assistant! I know there were many good candidates, some of whom promised not to put bite marks in the pencils. I'll make sure your time is only spent doing what's most important. For example, Wednesday's overbooked. I'll cancel your four o'clock root canal, or I can ask the dentist to meet us at the dog park. We'll tell her you had to prioritize. Also, whoever "gym" is, I'll tell him if he wants to see you it can be at a time other than five in the morning or not at all. I can politely explain that you don't wake up until the heater comes on. I also reset the heater to come on at noon. No reason to run it if we're still asleep. You'll find I'm the best thing to happen to your career—which is now that of a personal dog walker.

This is a great opportunity,
Roger

The caller's in a hold
Doggy: Roger

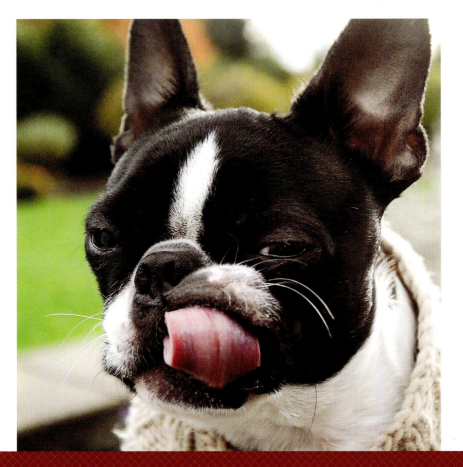

Arr, ye scurvy dog
Doggy: Riley

Dear Pack Leader of the Caribbean,

I see by my boating sweater that today's another pirates' adventure on the perilous high seas of Lake Poway, a San Diego County Park and Reservoir. Our seaworthy rental vessel will be infamous pedal boat nineteen. Makes a dog turn white with fear, with a mostly black face, just hearing the name. I can taste the salt from the freshwater cement lake and from that sunflower still stuck in my teeth. I found it on the backseat during the drive. Now I need a glass of water and some doggy dental floss to remove this shiver from me timbers. Does the ship's captain and sole source of propulsion mind if I use a string from this sweater? I realize it will ruin the sweater. Sometimes a pirate doggy must accept that this high seas adventure is really an hour of watching you take a spinning class. Let's just get a refund. We can plunder it or go through the drive-through.

I call the fries at the bottom of the bag!
Riley

Dear Unplugging and Replugging Pack Leader,

I, too, am moved by the sad tragedies of life, like having to wait through a firmware update before our *Dog Whisperer* Netflix binge. But this sad face actually began as my happy face. I adapted after realizing it's impossible for humans to see my sullen snout and not project their problems. In the grocery store a woman saw me and said, "Look at that sad dog. I bet he is trying really hard to cut carbs." Even when my tail wagged, people asked, "What's wrong, little doggy? Did your teenager come home from the groomer with a Mohawk?" At first I wasn't sure I'd like being a source of so much canine commiseration. But then I realized after a human's phone drops a call, I'm often given a belly rub. If they call back and it goes to voicemail, I might even get a treat. I'm essentially a therapy dog who doesn't have to wear an ugly vest.

I'm only truly saddened by your sweatpants,
Roxy

I'm happy to be sad if it'll make you happy
Doggy: Roxy

How do I love thee?
Doggy: Gronk

Dear Passion-Challenged Pack Leader,

Learning the proper way for a doggy to express himself is very important to becoming part of his human family. It's a lot like understanding the difference between what you should do on your family's expensive indoor rug as opposed to the neighbor's lawn. You have to know what goes where. Unfortunately, it seems that I'm doing something right here on your leg best reserved for couch cushions and occasionally to scar a child for life during a sleepover. I apologize for my overenthusiasm. I was hungry, you fed me, and I went nuts. Speaking of nuts, mine were unknowing accomplices in this whole act. Don't take any anger out on them when I'm the one who thought this would bring us closer. I can see now that all I've actually done is make your spouse uncomfortable. You're taking it quite well, though. Thanks for just shaking it off.

Sorry I humped your leg,
Gronk

My Dearest Pack Leader,

It has been ten minutes since you gazed into my eyes and said, "I'm going to the store, Dave. Be a good doggy. I'll see you in a half hour." How my heart has ached for you during this interminable fortminute. Will you ever return? I fear I've lost you to the ravages of running errands. I know not which store you're at or if they have the right chew toys. Will I even recognize you when you get back in twenty minutes? Will the madness of midmorning traffic change you into some stressed-out shell of your former self?

I'm hopeful you'll return soon. Every minute of your absence only strengthens the force with which I'll knock the groceries from your hands as you try to get them into the house. Soon no chores will prevent you from petting your forlorn puppy.

Don't forget the chew toys,
Dave

Slumber is the only anesthetic for your absence
Doggy: Dave

Why is the hardwood being such a hard-ass?
Doggy: Thatcher

Dear Foul Floorboards,

I apologized the first time I accidentally peed on you. I also apologized to Pack Leader, and I even did some time in the kennel. A few hours later I come up to check on you and look for food in the garbage, and you won't let me take two steps without pulling my paws apart. I didn't make much of it until the next day when I pooped in pretty much the same spot. Pack Leader said it was his fault for leaving me alone. Later I come to check on you and pull on a loose bedspread string until it's an unwoven mound of thread, and you won't let my feet work. Pack Leader just admitted that he cosmically crapped on you through me! I hope to grow old sleeping on your sunniest spots, but if this keeps up I'll refuse to have my claws clipped until they have no choice but to resurface you into sawdust. Next time I accidentally get you steamed, remember that you're covered in toilets, and some balloons would rather die against the ceiling than spend a second with you.

I'd still like to go steady,
Thatcher

Dear Shot-Pounding Pack Leader,

Why am I defying dog gravity just to await the gaze of your basset hound bloodshot eyes? The better question is why aren't you in bed? I lick your face for work in less than an hour! Where were you? Why do you smell like our mechanic's pants? Don't say you came in while I was sleeping. If we went upstairs, you know we'd find only one wiener-sized warm spot. I've been fast asleep all night worried you may never come home. I had to snuggle under the pillows because there was no one to let me steal their covers. You basically left me for dead. I tossed and turned for about five seconds, then dreamt I was being chased by a huge tsunami until my bladder heard the garage door. My water bowl's been empty since afternoon and you'll have to flush the toilet to refill it. We'll see if I even remember what else I wanted to bark about after I exorcise the Freddy Krueger tsunami that jumped from my dream to my bladder.

Next time have him bring a dog for your friend,
Goober

I waited up for you
Doggy: Goober

I am Thor, God of Likes
Doggy: Thor

Dear Pack Leader and President-Elect of the KISS Fan Club,

I do love you, but I can't accept a lecture on making good choices from a Pack Leader with a chest tattoo of O. J. Simpson. Unlike you, my spot won't sag. Poor O. J. grows increasingly sullen as your man boobs begin to bud. The universe sent a text right to my face! To you it sent a lifetime supply of undershirts. You worry that my one-in-a-million heart-emoji marking will have humans confusing me for a dog demigod. Why is that bad? A generation who does nothing but text and look at funny animals *should* worship an emoji-anointed Dalmatian. Although we could end up with a line of moms at our door begging me to use my supernatural saliva to lick back the boogers of their sniffling children. If a woman doesn't have any kids I'll lick her across the stomach and tomorrow she will. Have faith in Thor, Pack Leader. I'll also find you a farsighted female soul mate who just loves your tattoo of Nelson Mandela.

Eye heart you 4evr 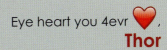,
Thor

Dear Thermometer-Popping Pack Leader,

I love having your extended pack over for Thanksgiving! It's the one meal where I can sit under the table and take in your family's collective foot-funk like a healing salve to my overly sanitized snout. So you can understand how horrified Truman doggy was to notice this puddle of turkey piddle. I know it smelled like aromatic meat drippings destined for gravy, but it looked too much like the real thing not to instinctively clean it up. Can you imagine if guests saw the turkey wasn't even gracious enough to use the bathroom before being plucked? You'd be mortified! A pool of juice drippings would probably form under you at that very moment. The teenagers would joke about the tinkling turkey, and then for the first time ever you'd have more leftovers than fridge space. Next year our ears will ring with the sound of crunching exoskeletons as your survivalist sister-in-law serves her traditional Thanksgiving feast of fried crickets and tap water. I *had* to lick the cutting board, or next year the only thing we'd be thankful for would be a travel-halting snowstorm.

I do taste the tarragon,
Truman

Who's responsible for the leak?
Doggy: Truman

Dog date afternoon
Doggy: Clyde

Dear Pepperoni-Digesting Pack Leader,

It's time you settled down with a nice female who will eventually get sick of pizza. You're not a kid anymore. You're now an accomplished adult male with many video game high scores and an impressive collection of cheat codes. It's time to meet someone who enjoys jogging and eating more than just one food.

    Don't come out of a sit, but see that woman in the pink scarf checking me out? She's perfect! She'll never eat pizza for fear of sauce staining her scarf. I'm going to jump out of the window and pretend to play in traffic. She'll try to lasso me with her scarf, but you'll bring me under control. She'll be impressed, and soon I'll be eating what's left of an omelet from the trash can she asked you to empty.

                  She celebrates her birthday on Super Bowl Sunday,
Clyde

Dear Lunch-Packing Pack Leader,

If I happen to collide with you every time you're making lunch, it's my job to then eat that piece of ham the impact sent free-falling toward the lawless international waters of the kitchen floor. Or else we'll have pirates! There's one out here chewing through a wire in your car. Also, *pirates* was the old term. Now we just call them rats.

I'll just advise through the cat's dung-smuggling tunnel. Use tons of mayo on Billy's sandwich. He'll throw it behind his bed before school. (Guess who cleans that if I'm out here?) For Maria, your preteen daughter, it's pizza day, and all the other moms are letting their kids buy lunch. Make sure you send her with a tuna sandwich aromatically disruptive enough to free up her next five years of weekends. Bless your ringworm-free heart for believing she won't just spend her allowance. If she forgets to throw the sandwich away or give it to the impoverished English teacher, Jet will find a very healthy snack in his bowl while Pack Leader is at yoga.

There's a baby carrot by your foot,
Jet

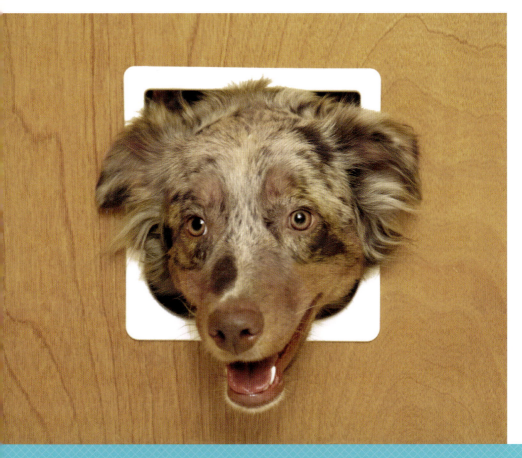

Make sure you cut the crusts off
Doggy: Jet

I don't know who you are anymore
Doggy: Maddy

Yo, Emcee Pack Leader!

This was supposed to be our first private time since we both got stuck under the house. Your wife took your pimply puberty puppies to her mom's house, and I thought we'd naturally spend it watching family comedies and seeing who can eat until the exact moment they fall asleep. Maybe you'd let me use the hot tub if you can turn it down to a temperature that doesn't make me pee. Instead you're blasting rap music and throwing Nerf footballs around in your underwear! It almost seemed fun until you broke a lamp. That scared me right back to my Maddy mat. I'm glad you cleaned it up, but why did you first have to put on a Viking helmet and hammer the fractured lamp stand into priceless heirloom powder? Why did you keep yelling, "I hate sweet potato fries, Dolores!"? Please return to the dorky Pack Leader who quietly does crosswords on the hammock. This music's so bad it makes me dream of hearing the vacuum cleaner. I need a Pack Leader who makes me feel safe. Right now I feel about as safe as that lamp.

It belonged to her Danish great-aunt,
Maddy

Dear Purr-Preferring Pack Leader,

If there's something you need to tell me, I just want you to know that I'll always love you. You're my forever Pack Leader, but I'd be disloyal if I didn't tell you this costume is a serious indicator of cat curiosity. Trust a dog who's done shelter time and met about every breed. If a bare dog isn't silly enough for a human, it's only a matter of time before he's fancying some feline who frequently forgets to suck its tongue in. You may not believe you love both cats and dogs based on the fact your trailer hitch is tastefully adorned with decorative testicles. Just know that it's okay. Sure, a dog can stop an intruder and save your life, while a cat will purr against his legs as he removes your TV from its wall mount. But I'd love to get a cat if it'll make you happy and free me of this Etsy abomination. All I ask is to please get another dog in case the cat tries to kill you and I need backup.

Say good-bye to your lizards,
Little B

Different strokes for different pig-Muppet mutants with wilted Mohawks

Doggy: Little B

Hard day at work?
Doggy: Dudu

Dear Patience-Testing Pack Leader,

Have you ever noticed that the later you come home, the longer I have to "work" for my treat? Do you know how hard it is for a dog to keep his taste buds from telling his teeth there's a cookie in his mouth? Every moment feels like an eternity—four eternities in dog years. Some days the treat tastes so good, I have to think about leaf blowers and helium balloons to prevent premature chewing. How does this help us connect? Does your boss give you a paycheck only to keep you in a sit at the bank until he says you can approach the teller? If so, he sounds like the kind of maniac who'd pretend to throw you a bone but nothing ever leaves his hands. You're better off staying home and inventing sandals that secretly taste like chicken. We'd never have to work again! Are you ready to stop torturing yourself and finally taste what life has to offer?

"Okay" is the only right answer,
Dudu

Dear Pre-enrolling Pack Leader,

I'm not panting because I'm trapped in a dinosaur muzzle. I'm just panicked for my first day of puppy preschool. What was school like for you, Pack Leader? I hear to graduate you have to ignore a smell. Did you pass the sniff test? Who were your friends at school? Did you chase girls? Did you chase squirrels? Did you have to work hard every day not to jump out at skateboards during teenager training? Were you ever afraid of a bully bulldog hoarding the water dish? I think on the first day I should establish Rory's dominance by walking in and immediately biting the biggest dog on the butt. It worked at the dog park. The Pack Leader of that punctured pooch even remarked that I was more than ready for school. She said, "Your puppy will be happier when he learns all the rules." The first rule I'd like to learn is the one against dogs on swings.

My midterm is to swallow your watch,

Rory

Antisocial studies
Puppy: Rory

But I got you a coupon for a free bathroom cleaning

Doggy: Joseph

Dear Totally Pissed-Off Pack Leader,

Do you know how hard it is to do something nice for you? While you were napping it occurred to me that I've missed your past five birthdays because my reminders app crashed on my smartbone. So I decided to make you a coupon for one free bathroom cleaning where I will personally shine every surface, including emptying the trash (onto the living room floor). But my paw shakes when I write, so I just went ahead and started washing the toilet. As you can see by the paisley tongue-print designs smeared across the vanity mirror, I cleaned that as well. I was about to ask the cat to change the toilet paper when you saw me and yelled, "Joseph, you know better!" What I know is that my beloved Pack Leader has two jobs and neither one appears to be cleaning. Even a dirty dog likes his water bowl degunked. Your bowl is pristine. Or it was until you came in here.

I smell an alligator in your pipes,
Joseph

Dear Drifting-Apart Pack Leader,

I, too, miss our past puppy love. But now that I'm an adult doggy and you have a boyfriend, our relationship has actually blossomed into a deeper, more meaningful obligation to feed and shelter. If you're worried I'm going to create a profile on Plenty of Pack Leaders, I guess we could start developing more interests in common. Would you like to take a cooking class? I'd like you to. What about a dog-grooming workshop? We'll bond, and you'll get a great workout trying to trim my claws. We could try speed walking, provided you speed walk slow enough so I can smell and mark every bush. I'll do anything that brings us closer. We could even learn to make and then trample balloon animals. Growing my Pack Leader relationship means nothing is off the table, even if I'm beneath it shivering because you accidentally popped the poodle's tail.

Nothing's more intimate than expressing anal glands,
Whisky

Still crazy after all these dog years
Doggy: Whisky

When was the last time you took a shower?
Doggy: Roni

Dear Pants-Perforating Pack Leader,

As the fashion innovator behind pre-ripped denim, I know how much time it takes to figure out the perfect place to rip next season's jeans. But you haven't moved in weeks and your test pants aren't even frayed. A walk might inspire you. I'll join you if you want. And you look thinner than a meth-addicted whippet. Let's walk over to that dog-friendly café for breakfast. I'll have whatever you drop. Please order and drop a side of sausage. Also be sure to sit near a water dish so I can top off my bladder before we leave. On the way home I'm going to pee on a tree belonging to a belligerent mastiff. He's so territorial he growls at passing clouds. When he tries to bite me, I'll hide behind you and the next thing you know your jeans will be irrigated with inspiration.

Pick a hole that helps you scratch the stitches,

Roni

Dear Pack Puppy Brother Evan,

Pack Leader gave me specific instructions for your bath. I'm to jump in, snap at soap bubbles until I catch one, then dig in the water until you and the entire bathroom floor are completely drenched. Then we are to get out, run past the towels to shake next to the recently cleaned windows, and finally remove any remaining moisture by going outside to roll in dirt. Pack Leader said nothing about snorkeling, scuba, or any underwater activities. If she asks, "Scruffy, all done with the bath?" I'll have to bark "no" because Evan and I have been feeding the imaginary sea turtles who live in the sunken toy motorboat. I love turtles, both real and imagined, but tub time isn't turtle time. If we're caught, tell her this thing on my head is for underwater toe licking. Don't tell her we spent our entire bath exploring the Galápagos. I don't want the cat to start doing your baths. He'll just lick half your head before deciding he's dirtier.

I'll make sure you're poorly rinsed and forever itchy,
Scruffy

Tub brothers
Puppy: Scruffy (with Evan)

Bark at the moon
Doggy: Ozzy

Listen, Foster Pack Leader,

I can tell you're a really nice woman, but I want you to know I won't be hurt if we can't make this work. My previous Pack Leader thought it would be cool to train me to bark at naked humans. I ended up at the shelter when a neighbor remarked to Pack Leader's wife that "Ozzy must've really hated your new cleaning lady. The minute she arrived he barked for two straight hours." Since this is the first time I've seen you get out of the shower, it's probably good to break the news that Ozzy barks at butts. They tried trainers at the kennel but nothing changed. I even met a real dog whisperer, but the kennel was so full of barking I couldn't hear a word he said. I hope one day there's a cure. Until then, you'll have to accept you can never take me to a South American beach.

I like your tattoo!
Ozzy

Dear Purple-Lipped Pack Leader,

Why haven't you gotten in the pool yet? Are you getting cold feet just because it's the middle of winter and if you take your shoes off you'll actually get cold feet? I double-dog promise you'll go numb in no time and forget about the huge "No dogs in the pool" sign they installed a week after we moved in. It's their fault for posting a sign no dog can read. I actually thought it said "Dogs *required* to pee in the pool." I don't care if the condo association lady fines you like last time I traded my leash for some low-impact cardio. Tell her I made nationals in the Olympic Bad Breath Stroke. Tell her I just hatched from a submerged cocoon. Who cares? No one's here but us, and we won't get in trouble. Where are you going?

If I get caught I won't say I know you,
Lilly

The water's actually quite warm in spots
Doggy: Lilly

Oh boy, we're getting evicted!
Doggy: Shanna

Dear Overdraft-Protecting Pack Leader,

While you were at work, your new friends came over to help you with my surprise. You didn't tell me we were moving! Thank you. How exciting. You did a great job keeping it a secret. Are we going to live at the park? I've always wanted my house to also be a bathroom. How about we move to Madagascar and see if I can get lemur work? We can do anything without an apartment keeping us tethered (or warm and dry). Let's take a road trip. We'll be living in our car anyway. It'll be so much fun to park in a new place every night. Eventually we'll choose a new apartment. This time let's start with an open floor plan so I don't have to eat the walls while you're at work.

I'll wait in the car,
Shanna

Dear Stuck-in-the-Bathroom Beta,

Given Heidi doggy's status as undisputed Pack Leader and bed hog, I decided I'll be the one to help you socialize our foster doggy, Schmidt. I truly want to help because I love all doggies. Also, I think Schmidt's kennel served lead kibble. Do you know he barked at a baby? He said that the infant took his teething ring! I had to shove our faces into these decaf caramel lattes abandoned by a pod of texting teens before any other babies started looking familiar.

Next time please check before leashing me to a dog who suffers from paranoid teething-toy psychosis. He's not ready for people. We need to start him on kittens. When he stops accusing them of stealing his ten-speed, we'll consider another public outing. Right now it's a long time until he's back at nice places like a Starbucks in a Safeway.

He asked if I know your Social Security number,

Heidi

Socializing Schmidt
Doggy: Heidi the Aussie (with Schmidt the Foster Lab)

Mona Lisa had peanut butter stuck to her gums
Puppy: Jess

Dear Picasso-Faced Pack Leader,

Let me just explain right here at the beginning of our relationship that it only *appears* like all I do is eat, sleep, play, and poop. A human will never appreciate the toll it takes on a puppy to forever be the cutest anything anywhere. You couldn't handle being mauled by teams of sniffling schoolkids who find you too adorable not to slime. I could see jealous babies forming a boycott, making it next to impossible to steal ice creams. That's why I'm always dog-tired. Also I'm not going to make it an issue, but there was never any discussion about stairs. You'll have to teach me how to use them and what to do if a cat's causing a roadblock.

I know you'll quickly become a good puppy parent. There was just something different about you during adoption day. It was the huge piece of hamburger you slipped me to prove to your kids I wasn't dead. That's when I knew you understood what I was looking for in a long-term relationship.

Let's renew our vows,
Jess

Dear Grandpa Pack Leader,

Has anyone told you that you might just be the most interesting human in the world? I'm surprised your grown kids don't call you every day just to hear you tell the one about the flat tire you got in a Mississippi rainstorm. I love the part where you get out of the car and the rain stops, plus it turns out your tire's fine. That's the kind of anticlimactic ending a dog never gets tired of not being startled awake by. Your kids have heard the story so many times that no matter where they are or what the weather is like, they'll never mention rainstorms or Mississippi. If it's sunny they just say, "It's clear." Your grandkids laugh when you stab a sack of flour with a bayonet on the Fourth of July. I think it shows character and good judgment. I don't care that you always smell like those birds who eat fermented berries. I love watching you wake up wondering which room you're in. It means you'll probably forget and feed me two breakfasts.

These are your best years of my life,
Rusty

I would LOVE to see your collection of complimentary hotel soaps!
Doggy: Rusty

Diets require sacrifice

Doggy: Ellie

Dear Portion-Controlling Pack Leader,

I'm not some dog you adopted just to eat fallen bits of food before they attract ants. I'm your new personal fitness instructor, and I'm here to get you off the couch to take me for a walk! I'm so dedicated that on your last trip to the kitchen, I actually peed on your couch, despite being housebroken. I'm a master motivator, and I can tell by how you're cursing and looking for my leash that you are already much more enthusiastic about getting some exercise.

I've also licked all your popcorn and devoured the potato chips in the pantry, and as your ASPCA-registered doggy dietician I promise to protect you from any fattening human foods left on an easily accessible shelf. My big slobber globules on your salty snacks should help you disassociate from the pleasure these foods give you.

Actually, eating all your popcorn's made me drowsy. Since I've already peed, let's skip to the next lesson where I curl up on my new couch for five hours to demonstrate the importance of getting enough rest.

Results guaranteed!
Ellie

Dear Pack Guru,

I do not want to go in the dog run every time company comes over. I just love meeting new people so much I forget to measure where my nose ends and their crotches begin. Please help me relax. I tried drinking, but I always ended up frantically banging my butt against the back door with the pained grimace of a dog about to commit a major party foul. Teach me to meditate and achieve the peace you found after you saw that cricket die beneath a pile of broken plates. You were so distraught you didn't even care that it actually *was* my old tennis ball I smelled behind the china cabinet.

How do we start, Pack Leader? Yes, I am imagining a place I feel safe and warm—it's on your bed where I'm not allowed. Now I'm imagining you yelling at me to get down. Yes, I actually can feel sand under my paws. I'm imagining taking a crap in your kid's sandbox. Imagining? I mean remembering. I remember that it was not the best time to focus on your breath.

I imagine I'll get used to the dog run,
Sizemore

Now imagine yourself *not* knocking over the baby

Doggy: Sizemore

ACKNOWLEDGMENTS

First let me give gobs of infinitely gracious thanks to my stellar editor, Allison Adler, along with my awesome agent, David Fugate. I am furthermore deeply thankful for the design talents of Holly Swayne, the friendship and support of Lane Foster, Kathy Hilliard, and Patty Rice, and everyone at Andrews McMeel for their inspired development of this and all works. As always, thanks to my bro Andrew Norelli, and to the wonderful Monika Orrey for her continued support and friendship. My deepest appreciation and love to my wife of twenty years, Barbara, and my sons Ben and Seth. And above all thank you to all animal lovers with whom I get to share a smile.

PHOTOGRAPHER CREDITS

Lin Atril, Scruffy and Evan, page 47; Lenaea Ayala, Goober, page 23; Mary Baker, Rusty, page 59; Barie Barie, Heidi and Schmidt, page 55; Susana Boglione, Roger, page 11; John Bryant, Truman, page 27; Nancy Canty, Maddy, page 32; Neil Davis Jr., Ellie, page 60; Elaine Dudzinski, Ozzy, page 48; Josh Dufur, Thatcher, page 20; Anne Fearon-Wood, Clyde, page 28; Christina Frett, Little B, page 35; Gerardina Giannattasio, Whisky, page 43; Joel Hawkins, Jet, page 31; Martin Hill, Jess, page 56; Josie Hopkins, Riley, page 12; Stuart Howe, Dave, page 19; Laura J., Joseph, page 40; George Landon, Oreo Cookie Crumb, page 8; Nick's Photography, Thor, page 24; Kristi Orlando, Roxy, page 15; Vanessa Privett, Rory, page 39; Eva Prokop, Shanna, page 52; Carol Robinson, Nutmeg (a.k.a. Ladybug), page 7; Danielle Scott, Sizemore, page 63; Zhang Shenjie, Dudu, page 36; Santiago Stucchi-Portocarrero, Roni, page 44; Jan van Dijk, Lilly, page 51; Jeff Vize, Gronk, page 16.